# Parents & Kids
# Talking About
# School
# *Violence*

# Also from Boys Town Press

## *For Parents*

*Common Sense Parenting®* (also in audio and Spanish)

*Common Sense Parenting Learn-at-Home Video Kit*

*Angry Kids, Frustrated Parents*

*Boys Town Videos for Parents*

*Dealing With Your Kids' 7 Biggest Troubles*

*Unmasking Sexual Con Games: Parent Guide*

*Getting Along with Others: Activity Book*

## *For Teens*

*A Good Friend: How to Make One, How to Be One*

*Who's in the Mirror? Finding the Real Me*

*What's Right for Me? Making Good Choices in Relationships*

*One to One: Listening Tapes on Dating, Alcohol, Suicide and More*

*Unmasking Sexual Con Games: Student Guide*

**For a free Boys Town Press catalog, call 1-800-282-6657.**

A BOYS TOWN
How-To Book

# Parents & Kids
# Talking About
# School
# *Violence*

Val J. Peter
Executive Director, Boys Town

BOYS
TOWN
PRESS

# Parents & Kids Talking About School Violence

Published by the Boys Town Press
Father Flanagan's Boys' Home
Boys Town, Nebraska 68010

## Publisher's Cataloging in Publication
### *(Prepared by Quality Books Inc.)*

Peter, Val J.
   Parents & kids talking about school
violence : a Boys Town how-to book / Val J. Peter.
--1st ed.
   p. cm.
   ISBN: 0-938510-74-6

   1. School violence--Prevention. 2. Parent and teenager. 3. Anger in adolescence. I. Title.

LB3013.3.P48 2000                    371.7'82
                                     QBI99-1605

10   9   8   7   6   5   4   3   2   1

*Parents and children can
call the Boys Town National Hotline
for help with any problem,
24 hours a day, every day.*

# Table of Contents

# Introduction

We at Boys Town know how to make schools safe.

When kids come to us, they hate school. Our kids have been victims of some of the poorest schools in America. They have not been taught. They have been passed from grade to grade. They have been allowed to fight. They have been allowed to mouth off to teachers. They have been allowed to bully one another and to do all the things that make schools places that are unhappy and unsafe.

Safety is like freedom. It is not something someone gives you. You, as parents, have to actively help create it. There are various simple means of being energetic, caring, sharing parents.

I remember as a young boy reading the works of James Fenimore Cooper such as *The Pathfinder, The Deer Slayer,* and *The Last of the Mohicans.* And I especially remember reading how young Native-American boys were taught by their parents how to read the signs of nature – the signs of danger and the signs of warmth and safety. They learned the secrets that were hidden in every leaf and rock. It was wisdom that was passed down among the Native Americans from parents to children.

We need to teach our boys and girls how to read the signs of danger and the signs of safety within schools. It is a similar wisdom we need to pass on to our children on how to make schools places of learning, places of fun and of safety.

These chapters were written to share with you the secrets we have learned at Boys Town – secrets of wisdom hidden in every school building across America if we will only look for them.

It is also good to remember that one of the benefits of discussing school safety with your child is that by doing so you develop greater communication between the two of you. That's a real benefit.

If you learn to communicate successfully in the area of school safety, there will be an added encouragement to communicate between the two of you on other issues even more important than this. In a sense, school safety is a nice, neutral issue to use to improve communication skills while at the same time helping your child feel closer to you.

So there is a double benefit. Please share this little book with others.

# For
# Parents

# What to Tell Your Children About School *Violence*

There can be some very positive things that happen if you sit down and talk with your child about the horrible events in Littleton, Colorado, Paducah, Kentucky, or Conyers, Georgia.

First of all, parents cannot pretend incidents of school violence don't happen. Think of the parent-child opportunity you will miss. It also is not a good idea to pigeon-hole the event into one explanation.

You will see this phenomenon of pigeonholing explanations happen in the media coverage over and over. A psychiatrist will say the whole thing is caused by mental illness. Pastors will say it is all caused by immorality. The police say that it is all a matter of breaking the law.

These violent events probably fill all of those categories and even more. But these explanations are not really helpful when talking to your child. Here are some very positive ways to help your child and yourself deal with these awful tragedies.

## *Deal* with the *Feelings*

Deal with the issue of teen deaths and violence on the emotional level – your child's emotions and your emotions.

■ Littleton and the other school shootings were scary. It is good to say to your child: "They scared me, too, and made me fearful."

■ It was horrible and sad. ("It made me sad, too.")

■ It was a tragedy, a disaster.

■ It was very bad. In other words, we can't assign a positive word to it. Let your children share their feelings as well.

■ Avoid the extremes of pretending it didn't happen on one hand while participating in the morbid fascination with pictures of bodies on the other hand. (Turn the television off when these kinds of "heightened journalism" appear.)

On the emotional level, deal with your child's fear. Common sense tells us there is a healthy kind of fear. Little children should develop a healthy fear of crossing the street without looking or of playing with matches. Adolescents should have a healthy fear of sinister-looking folks, whether they are in school or the shopping malls.

However, don't let fear run amuck. When fear becomes anxiety, it ruins the moment and prevents your child from enjoying life.

The bottom line is: A parent and child sharing emotions in a positive constructive way is not only healthy, it is also a blessed experience for both. When a child is very much afraid, then as a parent you must realize something has been taken away from your child. As a parent, you need to repair and replace it emotionally. What a terrific opportunity for a mom or a dad!

# *Share* **Thoughts**

As parents, it is good to share some thoughts with your children. Not much is clear in Littleton except the fact that the two kids who did these horrible deeds were very alienated. (By the way, it is okay to be mad at these kids.) Share with your children, in a very positive manner, how youth can become alienated in one of the following three ways:

■ **Alienation from parents** – Talk together about how you and your child have some real solid, positive relationships that are warm and caring. This doesn't mean your child is a "Beaver Cleaver;" it means he or she is not completely alienated. In other words, you have appropriate relationships with your child. Rejoice in them!

- **Alienation from peers** – Point out friendship skills your child has and how your child has good, positive, healthy friends. Rejoice in this!

- **Alienation from God** – Point out how your family prays together and relies on the Lord as a source of strength in times of trouble and a source of joy in good times. Point out to your child that your family has a memorable past, a worthwhile present, and a hopeful future. Point out that your family is not faithless or simply angry at everybody. Point out that all of you in the family have a conscience. These are all causes to rejoice.

Most importantly, don't take a normal child with normal fears to a therapist over this matter.

# **Bring**
## *Closure*

Go for closure. Wouldn't it be great if your child could go to school and say: "My parents and I had a long talk about this, and we did something about it. We said a prayer together, and we continue to pray every night for these families," or "We are making a memorial gift." It is okay for your child to attend a memorial service. It is all right for your child to hang out with his or her friends and discuss it.

However, don't make it a topic of discussion for days on end. Bring some closure to it. Get on with the business of being a child, being a family, being a student, and being a parent. Count your blessings.

# Get *Help*

Of course, if your child is alienated from family, peers, and God, the action taken needs to be drastic. In that case, call the Boys Town National Hotline at 1-800-448-3000. The Hotline is a nationwide toll-free resource and referral service for children and parents.

# Fixing Your Family:
# What to Do & How to Do It

Littleton, Colorado. Conyers, Georgia. Paducah, Kentucky. All raise questions in the minds of moms and dads about how things are going in their own families. Before you set out on a home improvement plan, try to gather some wisdom about what to do and how to do it.

# What *Not* to Do

When looking at your own family, it is very easy to beat yourself up. It is very easy to despair. Don't do it!

- It may seem clever to make an odious comparison between your home and a home where the kids' rooms are always in perfect order, where the grass never needs cutting, where the garbage is always taken out on time, and where peace and harmony dwell serene.

- However, it is good to look at our faults and failings and realize what they are. Sometimes we are in denial about them.

- But once we know our faults and failings, it doesn't really help to beat ourselves up too much or to despair.

- We need a realistic model of what a family should be like.

- Real families are like used cars. They are not like new models right off the assembly line.

- A good used car is serviceable, functional and is quite satisfying. It is something useful and something we like to keep.

- So let's avoid despair.

---

# A Realistic Model for *Family Life*

---

I like to start with moms and dads:

- We adults are built to care for, nurture, and protect our young. It is a species-specific behavior.

- That simply means that for human beings, caring for, nurturing, and protecting our young are characteristic behaviors.

- They may not be characteristic of certain fish or animals. But they are characteristic of this species called the human race.

- Feelings of self-sacrifice are species-specific to us.

- Human beings just don't flourish well without self-sacrifice or without caring and nurturing and protection.

- So a realistic model includes care, nurture, and protection of our children.

- A realistic model means that you and I as moms and dads need to get in touch with how good those feelings are.

If you are parenting for your needs, you won't enjoy it and you probably won't be successful.

- In other words, caring can't be dependent on expecting personal rewards.

Feeling good about parenting is not like feeling good about being the top Lexus salesman for the month. As top salesman, there are all kinds of external reinforcers: your picture on the bulletin board, a bonus in your paycheck, and the younger salespeople calling you "sir." Not so in parenting.

■ As a result of doing a good job as a mom or dad, don't expect your kids to put your picture on their bulletin board. Don't expect them, out of gratitude, to abstain from hitting you up for money. And don't expect them to tell their friends about what a good dad or mom you are.

■ What you get your satisfaction from is the caring, the nurturing, and the protecting behaviors you engage in. Human beings are built to feel good about those things, very good, indeed.

- It's great if Mom and Dad reinforce each other. You surely feel good about the progress your kids are making in school. And you feel good about the friendship skills they are using with their peers. But those feelings don't overwhelm us every day. So you mostly have to feel good about caring, nurturing, and protecting your kids.

- Don't forget that Mom and Dad have to settle their basic disagreements and their basic differences. If there is a leak in the crock, there will be no soup. If there is a crack in the cup, the coffee is spilled. If adults are in conflict, successful parenting evaporates.

## *Improving* the Family

When you set out on a family improvement process, strive for a middle ground.

Don't start with extremes. In other words, don't start with a sudden ill-advised scheme like this:

- ■ "I'm going to fix everything."

- ■ "I'm going to announce we will drive down to the lake and we are going to fish together this Saturday. That's all there is to it."

This is a recipe for failure. It's something like saying: "My life is not so good, yours is no good either. So we are going to do unpleasant things together." Instead, you should:

- ■ Relax, and go slow.

- ■ Begin with some humor. Humor is just the opposite of thinking about your family the way Anthony Quinn as Zorba the Greek described his: "The whole catastrophe."

- ■ Begin the way you did when your child was just born into the world.

- Remember how almost instinctively you picked up your child and tried to make him or her laugh.

- You were trying to make the child happy.

- You were not satisfying your own ego needs.

- That instinctive approach with your infant son or daughter is something you can rely on. Don't stop doing it when they are adolescents.

One of the keys to a successful family renewal program is to understand why things are the way they are right now.

- For example, if the family watches television during dinner, understand why. The TV fills the uncomfortable silence, a silence that is unsatisfying to everybody.

- The TV may not be much, but at least it's noise and something you can watch.

- Many people want to blame television for what we have done to ourselves.

- You can say that the TV is a problem. You can point your finger at it.

- You can take drastic action and remove it from the table.

- And if that's all you do, nothing good will happen.

- You need to begin to practice your conversation skills. You need to start encouraging table talk.

- You need to get your kids to buy in on communicating with one another and then preteach for a week or ten days. ("In ten days we start practicing our conversation skills at the table.")

- Remember that a typical childhood response to your question, "How was your day?" is for your child to say, Great" or "Okay" or "Nothing happened."

- So immediately follow up with a specific question: "What were your classes like?"

- It is possible to generate and sustain conversation with a teenager.

- It takes skill and kindness and persistence on your part.

- It's a skill that you can learn. In fact, it's a fun skill to learn. It's like debriefing someone.

- It's tough to get started, but once conversation starts, it sustains itself.

- Keep working at it. Think of yourself as a facilitator of the conversation.

In my house at Boys Town, kids eat with me every night, Monday through Friday. And I always start the conversation by going around the table and asking, "Tell us all something good that happened to you today." You have to facilitate the answer lest you get only grunts or "Nothing happened" or "Everything's fine, thanks." It takes time. It takes effort. But it does pay dividends.

So taking TV away from the supper table won't significantly change your family life. But it is a good start.

Be sure to praise your kids for taking part in the conversation. Be sure to enjoy the role of facilitator. I have found it to be a lot of fun. I like to do it; I like it a lot.

If you decide to plan a vacation, please remember the following:

- The first response from your teenager may be, "I don't want to go."

- Follow that with some empathy ("I understand how you feel") and encouragement ("I'm sure we'll have fun together"), not sarcasm and put downs.

- Try, if you can, to avoid a tour of the textile plants of North Carolina, the hog rendering works of Iowa, or the plentiful landfill sites of Southern California.

■ Some things are attractive to teenagers. The nation's capitol and the national parks are interesting. The beach, the mountains, and lakes are all fun places.

Finally, let's all try to learn the lesson about families that is taught in natural disasters and in hard times:

■ In disasters and hard times, families magically work together.

■ At such times, common generosity, concern, and helpfulness spontaneously rise to the top.

■ We willingly and readily set aside our petty concerns.

■ We put caring and sharing up front.

■ It feels good. It looks good. It is good.

- Outside these extreme conditions, pettiness will rise to the top unless we work at it.

In the end, there are two adages to always keep in mind:

- Excess analysis leads to paralysis.
- An extreme solution leads to family pollution.

# How Does *Media Violence* Impact Your Children?

Jack Valenti, president of the Motion Picture Association of America, says that Hollywood is not to blame for school shootings in particular and our violent culture in general. He says that only those who are "predisposed to violence" will be moved to violent acts by films filled with violence and gore.

On the other hand, many TV preachers say if there was no violence on television or in films, our problems would be pretty much solved.

Both are off the mark. Jack Valenti absolves Hollywood of responsibility. The TV preachers demonize the film industry and television.

Let's start with Hollywood.

Hollywood really needs to be confronted, not with all of the blame, but with its fair share of it, to be sure. And that's a lot!

# Getting 'Used' to *Violence*

In 1972 and 1982, there were surveys done by the Surgeons General of the United States showing clearly that violence on television contributes to violent behavior. And not just for those "predisposed to violence."

Let's take a look at how this happens. What we want to look at specifically is the phenomenon called "habituation:"

- Put simply, we human beings are designed to respond to strong stimuli.

- If there is a hog rendering plant with a strong smell near our home, we say, "Wow, what a stink."

- But if the smell continues over a long period of time, we stop perceiving it as strong and eventually we do not notice it anymore. We no longer say, "Wow, this place stinks."

- It's not a conscious decision on our part not to notice it.

- We can't much respond to it even if we want to.

- That's habituation.

So Hollywood can blab on and on about how many Americans see "no problem" with violent movies. But there is a problem. It is called habituation.

Does watching Leonardo DiCaprio's *The Basketball Diaries* have no effect on kids except for perhaps those who are "predisposed to violence?" Of course it has an effect on the general audience!

The U.S. Supreme Court recently allowed the family of a seriously wounded convenience store clerk to bring suit against Oliver Stone for the influence of his film *Natural Born Killers* on young people who imitated crimes depicted in the movie. Is the only damage done here when a person predisposed to violence commits a crime? Or are other kids harmed by watching it as well?

The answer, of course, is clear and straightforward: The more of these kinds of movies your children watch, the more habituated they become to violence. And the more desensitized they are to it.

- They don't see violence as wrong.

- They don't oppose it.

- They don't try to prevent it or stop it.

- They just don't care. They stand idly by. And their world gets more lonely, fearsome, and hostile.

- As Rhett Butler said to Scarlet O'Hara: "Frankly, my dear, I don't give a d---."

Is it harmful to society when a large number of children become desensitized or so habituated to violence that they just don't care? You bet it is.

- Kids should care about violence among peers. They should disapprove. They should say so. They should try to prevent it from happening. They should try to stop it when it occurs.

Does Hollywood need to take its share of the blame for this habituation? You bet it does.

- If it takes lots of lawsuits against various producers and studios so that the entertainment industry becomes aware of its responsibility, not just toward those predisposed to violence, but to all kids in general, then let's have more lawsuits. It's the American way.

- Many immigrants left their homelands for America to avoid raising their children in such violent societies.

On the other hand, even if there were no violence in films or on TV, that would not solve the problem of human violence. So it's an extreme position to demonize the film industry. The solution is not to shut down Hollywood. Everybody wants the product. Everybody also knows it's a little bad.

# What Is
# *Hollywood's Role?*

During bad times such as the epidemic of school violence, there is huge pressure on our society to point to one thing (in this case Hollywood), to condemn it and to move on. That is a contorted form of denial of the responsibility each and every one of us has to do something about stopping violence in our children's lives.

Demonizing Hollywood has a political aspect to it as well. Extremists on the right haul out kids and use them for all sorts of conservative agendas. When the agenda fades, the interest in these kids fades as well. That's not a general condemnation of conservatives. It's a condemnation of a peculiar tactic of extremists on the right. It's a solution that leaves individual parents off the hook. That's a bad idea.

Every single child who comes into the world and starts to grow has to fight the battle of lying, cheating, and stealing. The battle is for their minds and hearts. It is critical for their happiness and the good of the community that they win this battle. We all have to help them.

So, too, every single child who comes into the world and starts to grow has to fight the battle of violence – and win it. And we all have to help. If there are 60 million children, that means there are 60 million battles.

In regard to the violence in movies, the battle does not start when you take your kids to the movies. The battle starts when kids go to the movies on their own.

As executive director of Boys Town, I, too, am a parent like you. Some days I feel like the old lady who lived in a shoe, "who had so many children she didn't know what to do." I love them all. I don't put all the blame on Hollywood (or the Internet). But I do get mad at these industries for two reasons.

First, Hollywood is so selfish, caring so little for these, my kids. "We're not our brother's keeper," they keep saying. My kids are fighting their individual battles against violence, and Hollywood isn't helping.

Second, my kids and I often feel hemmed in by the environment. We often feel discouraged. We often feel that the world has gone far beyond our ability to respond. We feel like a Division II football team coming to play the Nebraska Cornhuskers. We feel we don't have a chance.

But that feeling is notoriously unreliable. We are David going out to meet Goliath. And David did win! So can we!

# The *Family's* Role

A parent's work with his or her children does have an impact. In fact, a parent's influence is the strongest influence on children. So you need to work with your kids with a sense of confidence.

My Boys Town kids tell me that what ruined their lives was not so much television, movies, or the Internet, as it was their parents' abandonment, betrayal, infidelity, drugs, alcohol, violence, and suicide. Not always, but all too often.

The battle for the minds and hearts of our children is being waged in our homes. We need to help our children win, one at a time. Every single child needs our help in winning this battle. The war is not lost. We can win. I remember the words from a

World War II song: "We did it before. And we can do it again."

It is true that our environment is increasingly anti-family. That's why Hollywood has to do its share to take responsibility instead of what Jack Valenti did: Whining and complaining it's only those who are "predisposed to violence" that we have to worry about. How about being honest and accurate, Jack? And Mom and Dad, how about being honest and open about your role in this, too?

# How to Learn and Teach Self-Control

Many of us remember our elementary school report cards that had a box entitled "Self-Control" or "Deportment." Its purpose was to let our moms and dads know we were coming along in growing up and in learning self-discipline. Here are some suggestions on ways to help your child learn self-control.

# *Parental* **Modeling**

Kids learn an awful lot about self-control or lack of self-control through what their parents do, especially in emotionally explosive situations:

■ As soon as some parents get behind the wheel of their car, they practice road rage.

■ Somebody cuts in front of them, and they begin to curse and swear.

■ In situations like this, your children watch you more intently than they watch a TV show.

Children learn a lot from that. A lot about self-control. Lack of self-control means lack of the ability to be civil.

- A boy gets his driver's license on his 16th birthday only to be involved in a fender-bender the next day.

- His father blows up, cursing and swearing, saying bad things about his son, the other driver, etc. Many parents are guilty of behavior like this.

- However, speaking calmly and acting rationally in this explosive situation is a great lesson in self-control to teach your son.

- It also builds trust.

For some people, a negative sports outcome ("my team lost") can ruin their day:

- "I feel mad because my team lost."

- "And I'm tempted to act mad as a result."

- Self-control, however, means that you can have the same negative opinion about how your team was coached and yet curb your tongue.

■ Otherwise, you are engaging in self-centeredness.

Remember when you were kids sitting around the family dinner table and Mom was "really mad?"

■ Signals would be passed eye to eye, from one kid to another.

■ "Mom's really mad; don't say a word."

■ Mom's frustration is like gasoline all over the garage floor, and you are tempted to throw a match on it.

There is a difference between facing a question about a valid issue and reacting to "trigger events." For example, a trigger event for you might include being reminded for the 400th time that you forgot Aunt Ethel's birthday 20 years ago or being deliberately baited with political comments everyone knows will enrage you. Self-control has to be learned for these trigger events.

■ Parents can model it.

■ It takes practice.

■ It's worthwhile.

Self-control is nothing more than feeling one way and acting in a different way for the good of all.

## Practice

Learning self-control is a matter of practice, practice, practice. You can't teach navigation in the middle of a storm. That's why you need to teach self-control in calm weather.

■ You first need to identify your road rage as very poor behavior.

■ You need to recognize that blowing up at your son for his fender-bender is poor behavior.

■ You need to identify that acting like a spoiled brat when your team loses is unacceptable behavior.

In other words, self-improvement starts with honest self-evaluation. After self-reflection and self-evaluation comes changing something in your life. Too many people think that self-improvement means adding something to their behavior but not changing any current behavior.

So a person starts on a diet by "eating absolutely everything I am already eating" and "walking just five minutes a day." Then he or she wonders, "How come I can't lose weight?"

To gain self-control and self-mastery, you really do have to change something in your life.

Change involves *regret* – identifying that what you are doing is inappropriate – and *willingness to change*. The next step is knowing *how* to change. There are many how-to books for parents out on the market. It is not hard to find one. Your child can learn a good self-control strategy (counting to 10, taking a deep breath, etc.), and so can you.

Remind your child that using self-control does not mean leading a miserable life.

- Self-control improves your day.

- It improves your relationships, and you feel better about yourself.

- Self-control leads to success in business, family, and other relationships.

- Self-control is a characteristic of a successful person.

- Self-control is about feeling good because you are acting good.

# Sibling *Relationships*

As a parent, also consider setting realistic goals for sibling relationships to give self-control a chance to grow. Write these rules in your house:

- **No horseplay.** Be sure that you are clear about what horseplay is – running in the house, wrestling, playing keep away, pushing, shoving.

- **No mean teasing.** Be sure to define what teasing is.

- **Teach self-control** as you have taught it to yourself.

- **Catch it happening, and reward it** when it does.

This will help children develop empathy for each other. And remind your child: "If you have a tinge of regret for what you did to your brother or sister, then you know for sure it was caused by your lack of self-control."

One last thought: Do not let your kids confuse self-control with stifling freedom. Self-control is the root of true freedom. True freedom is not letting yourself be a slave to your passions, not letting yourself be controlled by the whim of the moment. Self-control helps you be a kind, loving, and generous person.

# When *Bullies* *Threaten* Your Children

It is important to understand that our children often go to schools where there is a culture of violence. That doesn't mean that violent kids are coming to school every day and shooting everyone up. It means that there is an environment of intimidation and threats that makes the school a fearful place for your children – a place they would like to avoid.

# Examples from *History*

This is important to understand. In Nazi Germany, most of the citizens were not beaten up or dragged off to concentration camps. But it was a society that was oppressive in its constant threats to do so. People did not know who would report them on the slightest pretext or who would be the next victim.

In Soviet Russia during the Stalinist Era, most citizens weren't dragged off to the gulags in Siberia. But many were scared to the bone that it might happen to them or to one of their loved ones.

# *Bullying in School*

It is the all-enveloping environment of repeated threats and constant intimidation that make schools so fearful to so many kids. If your child is in one of these schools, spend time teaching him or her:

- How to avoid being a victim of violence.

- How to not go out looking for trouble.

- How to avoid attracting the attention of bullies.

The best self-defense to teach children in a school like this is not to arm them with fists or weapons, but rather to help them learn the skills of smart behavior, of not making themselves a target.

Remember that kids are trapped in high schools. As an adult, you are usually not trapped in your job. You can always move to some other company. But in many cases, students cannot move to other schools.

Most environments of intimidation, however, are less than total.

Let's say, for example, that your child goes to a school where there is some bullying, but it isn't all pervasive. Let's say that your child was bullied. Perhaps he or she unsuspectingly did something to attract the bullies' attention, was threatened badly and is very scared. This is a case of incidental bullying.

Parents here are often times tempted to jump in and be bigger bullies than the bullies at school.

- They instantly overreact.
- They want to get a lawyer.
- They want to sue the school.
- They make a total nuisance of themselves.

■ They give their kids very bad role-modeling by acting like bullies themselves.

Other parents may look at their child as being "a little wimpy." Dad wants his son to be a bully, to fight and to win, to be the tough guy.

■ This is teaching our kids to be bullies.

■ Then they can join the bullying group.

■ When that son grows up and becomes a father, he will probably be a bully to his own family too.

■ That is not a good solution.

# What You *Can Do*

The better solution is to teach your son or daughter the skills he or she needs not to look for trouble. (If your home is on the edge of a swamp, it's good to teach your children to have a healthy respect for alligators.) You can also teach your child how to develop positive relationships with peers.

Parents need to understand that children who have been bullied probably feel inadequate and very much filled with shame – lost, powerless: "They took my books." "They took my lunch money." "One of them punched me." You can help your children get through this emotional trouble.

- Teach children the skills they need to avoid trouble.

- Teach children the skills they need to learn to make friends.

- Teach your children that although there may be "bears in the forest," it is still a good place to go camping if they take certain precautions.

Parents must also understand that you cannot solve the problems your children have within their peer group.

■ Kids have to sort it out themselves.

■ Parents can be supportive.

■ A bully will put your child in the emotional state of being very scared, with feelings hurt.

■ You can help your son or daughter through these emotional states.

■ You need to bring it up: "You don't look good. You look worried."

■ As a parent, offer your help.

■ Teach coping skills.

One of the best things that you can teach your son or daughter is: "These things too shall pass."

■ Most bullying is done verbally rather than physically.

- There is a natural period of brutality in some young people.

- Most bullying disappears by the time kids go to college or enter the work world.

- In other words, it usually gets better.

- However, some childhood bullies remain bullies all their lives.

- They usually end up very isolated and unhappy, often in big-time trouble with the law.

Bullying doesn't occur just when our kids are in school. There will be instances of bullying in their adult lives. Teaching them while they are still young how to deal with it in a positive way is to prepare them for a much happier adult life. It is really worth it.

# *How to Talk to* Your Parents About School *Violence*

This message is for the youth of America – how to talk with your mom or dad about the issues of school violence.

Before all else, remember this: If you are engaged in fringe behavior or belong to a dangerous or violent group, it is time to seek help. Yes, if you are in danger yourself or are putting others in danger, then respond to your parents positively. Let them help you.

Even if you feel your relationship with them is weak, please, let them help.

It is good to remember that when your parents sit down and talk to you about a school tragedy like Littleton, don't choose this particular conversation to be defiant. That's right. Don't choose this particular conversation to be a jerk. Choose to do that some other time. Choose some other time to say: "I am 16 years old, and nobody is going to tell me what to do."

In other words, take this time to listen and cooperate. You will find it worthwhile to do. You will like yourself better if you do this.

Let's look at three things that are important as you talk to your parents.

# Your Parents Are *Scared*

Your parents would not be talking to you if they were not afraid. They would not be talking to you if what has happened in Littleton and other schools across the country did not make them fearful. Remember that. This kind of fear is healthy and good. So it's okay for you to be scared, too. It's no fun to talk about this, but it's okay to admit to yourself privately that it's scary. Maybe even your own school is scary. Don't minimize what happened in so many other places; don't think, "Such things could never happen in our school." And don't glorify it either: "Yo man, those dudes were cool."

And yes, you would gain attention by talking about making bombs or looking up how to make them on the Internet. But remember, it is breaking the law to yell

"Fire" in a theater. (And neither can you talk about bringing bombs on a plane, or taking rifles to school. There's a taboo on this.)

So realize your parents are scared and that it's okay for you to be scared, too.

# Your Parents May *Overreact*

You need to realize that if your parents are frightened enough, they may excessively intrude into your life for a time. They may take a sudden interest in your CDs, your video games, and your clothing. It may be misdirected concern, overblown and out of proportion to what is really going on in your life. But this is the time for you to stay calm and reassure your parents in a positive way that you know the difference between some of the lyrics on your CDs and what's appropriate and real.

You need to reassure your parents that at times you say things to show off – things you really don't mean, things that make your friends laugh, things they also know you don't mean. Remember that your parents are motivated to protect you.

# Practice *Cooperation*, Not Overreaction

Maybe your parents haven't been this concerned for a number of years. Maybe they haven't asked you in a long while about the music you listen to or the movies you go to or the friends you keep. (Even you may have to admit that a few of your friends are "a little weird.") This is not the time for manipulating your parents. It is not the time for getting unreasonably upset.

Your parents might temporarily invade parts of your life that they appropriately gave up looking into some time ago as you moved into adolescence. Be patient about that. Be cooperative. This will pass.

But there also may be things that your parents stopped doing such as asking where you were when you went out on certain occasions. It may be very appropriate for them to start attending to things they have neglected.

Remember that when you were a child, it was appropriate to tell them in advance where you were going. And even though you are now a teenager, it is still appropriate for them to ask where you have been. It's really not out of line at all. This is the time for cooperation. It's a time for maturity on your part. It's a time to show love to your parents.

Yes, you will hear things that you don't want to hear. Some of them appropriate and some of them not so appropriate from your parents. It's a time, as I said, for cooperation.

Two extremes are to be avoided with regard to privacy in your room. It is not appropriate for you to expect that your parents are never allowed into your room. There are occasions when they have every right and duty to be there. On the other hand, it is inappropriate for your parents to be in your room constantly poking around and searching for everything that is going on in there.

There is a middle ground in privacy for an adolescent. It is good to remember that.

Your parents have to make sure you are not making bombs. So don't feel violated. That's an overreaction. Use the skills that you have. And just as your parents have to be patient when you overreact, so you need to be patient when they overreact. This is not the time for either you or your parents to be unreasonably upset. In other words, no harumphing. No rolling of eyes. No sighing. No snotty remarks. It's a time for maturing.

Please don't feel you are being punished because your parents are worried and persist in demonstrating their worries. Identify some needed skills such as staying calm or letting your parents know where you are going and use them. You will never regret it.

In short, as a sign of maturity and general good nature, assure your parents that you are not engaging in fringe or dangerous behaviors. Avoid lying to them. Avoid making this an opportunity for a pitched battle.

# Time to *Build* More *Trust*

When incidents of youth violence occur, parents are likely to be upset and worried. Are you generally where you said you would be? Remember that trust is like a commodity or a product. Have you been producing it in reasonable amounts for your parents? If you have, it's a good time to pat yourself on the back. If you have not, it's a good time to reflect on your behavior.

Finally, after talking with your parents, have you left them feeling okay? Or are they upset because you wouldn't or couldn't assure them that you are not on the road to violent or destructive behavior?

If you are surprised at the lack of trust that your parents seem to have in you, how do you react? Has this made you realize, for the first time maybe, that it's time to build more trust? This is a great opportunity. Don't pass it by.

Before you finish talking with your mom or dad, why not say a little prayer together. The Lord's help is like glue that helps the family stick together.

And at the end, let your mom or dad give you a big hug. It may be the first one in a long time. It's important.

# What to Do When You Are *Disrespected*

Schools are meant to be places of learning, involvement, and positive common experiences. By almost every measure, kids who get involved in school activities do better academically, socially, and in just about every other way.

But in recent years, schools have changed drastically – for the worse. The quality and quantity of negativity has increased to dangerous levels, and it is tolerated. There have always been cliques of various sorts. But that is not the problem. Once schools began to tolerate more abusive language and more violent behavior, these schools became combat zones. Students become warriors. They gathered to victimize other groups.

So obsessed have educators become with student rights that the educational community suffers in two ways. First, not as much learning takes place. Second, schools are now places of alienation and violence.

The basic brotherhood and sisterhood of youth is fragmented and seems to have disappeared. Certain experiences that previously unified the student body, such as sports teams or theatrical events, no longer do so. There is an escalation of negative behavior, even open warfare among gangs.

Let me suggest four things that students can do when they are disrespected in school.

# *Actively* Ignore the Disrespect

Disrespect has two components: one external and the other internal. Externally you should just not attend to the disrespect. Actively ignore it. That means get yourself out of the situation. Consider the source. Say nothing. Leave. You will extinguish the behavior by doing this.

Another way to actively ignore disrespect is to avoid it. For example, if a certain hostile group hangs around a particular corner and hassles anyone who walks by, the best thing to do is not to walk by that corner.

When I was growing up, a group of bullies used to hang around the corner drugstore right after school. If you didn't want to be hassled, you went to the drugstore at a different time.

Now you may say that this is not fair and it's not what is supposed to happen. That's all true. But the real power is not what the bullies do, but what you do in response. Actively ignoring or avoiding disrespect is a clever thing, indeed.

---

# Don't Let *Disrespect* Hurt You

---

Sometimes, a student can't help but be hurt inside from the disrespect he or she receives from fellow students. Any youth cannot help but feel hurt deep down inside if he or she is unskilled athletically, or uncoordinated, or overweight. Disrespect in these situations doesn't just hurt. It hurts deep down inside.

When this happens, seek guidance from a caring, loving adult. In many cases, a wise adult can help someone who is a little overweight dress more appropriately. They can help an uncoordinated youth learn some sports-related skills.

Adults also can help you learn friendship skills. Oh, yes, you'll have to work harder to find friends. But you will find them, you will make them, and you will be happy.

I always remember a girl here at Boys Town who was born without a right hand. Yes, life was unfair. But it sure didn't bother this young girl. She sought guidance from adults. She knew that not all people are equal or full of the same potential. However, she made the most of what she had. She made many friends. She had a smile on her face. She was very well liked.

Look at the adult world. You'll discover that it is not just the homecoming king and queen who get married. Most people do. And most people do so happily. Most people find lifelong friends. So there is hope. The pain you feel inside from the disrespect won't last forever. So take courage.

---

# Don't Bring *Disrespect* on Yourself

---

Remember this:

- If you dress like a "trenchy," talk like a "trenchy," and act like a "trenchy," you will be treated like a "trenchy."

- If you dress like an outcast, are rude and obnoxious, you will bring much disrespect upon yourself.

- If you look like a "ho," act like a "ho," talk like a "ho," you will be treated like a "ho."

So don't go out of your way "to" engage in fringe and dangerous behaviors.

# *Give Respect* to Others and to Yourself

There isn't a kid who doesn't some-times feel angry at the world. There isn't a kid who doesn't feel at times that he or she is being treated unfairly. A recent article in *The Washington Post* quoted a suburban high school "trenchy" as saying: "In the seventh grade, I withdrew from people. I didn't have any friends. I started doing bad in school. I was probably more depressed. Then it kind of developed into anger. I just kept my distance."

This person did not respect himself. He let the alienation grow and grow until he began to engage in marginal and dangerous behavior. Don't let it go that far. If your negative feelings toward yourself and others are hurting your grades or your social life, get some help and get it right away.

An unfortunate strategy some kids who feel disrespected use is what I call "rejecting the rejecters." People who do this think this way:

- "I didn't make the football team, so football is a dumb sport and all the people who made the team are idiots."

- "I really wanted to sing a solo in the school play, but didn't get selected, so the school play, all the kids in it, the teachers, everyone, is dumb and stupid and now the butt of my jokes. I seek to destroy the play and the people associated with it. I was hurt, and now I want to hurt them back."

- "I wasn't invited to a party, so I'll try to ruin the party. If I blame a person for rejecting me," (my perception, remember, which can be faulty) "then I might try to do some damage to them by spreading mean rumors or harmful talk."

A really bad tendency is for your "rejection" to spread beyond a few things to everything – all of school, anything and everything. Worse is when "anti" groups form – groups whose unwritten code and behavior is to massively reject everything and everybody. Their activities can feed the revenge appetite, and what start as pranks and practical jokes turn into attack missions.

Much of this is simply a reaction to perceived rejection gone wild and dominating the life of an individual. Joy is gone, fun is perverted to "getting even," friends become scarce unless you find other "anti" people, and then life becomes "sick."

There is an old saying: "Smile and the world smiles with you. Cry and you'll cry alone." There's a lot of truth in that. Go for what will solve this problem. Make it better.

In conclusion, every one of us has been disrespected at times in our lives. There are certain things we can do to minimize this disrespect so that we can get on with the positive side of our lives.

There is an old Chinese proverb: "You cannot keep the bird of sorrow from flying over your head, but you can keep it from nesting in your hair."

Good advice.

# How to Avoid Using *Violence*

Just as we have to learn how to avoid being victims of violence, so, too, we have to learn how to avoid using violence to get our way. People who use violence to get their way are called victimizers. They are getting their needs met in antisocial violent ways. Boys and girls need to learn how to get their needs met in prosocial ways. They need to learn, in other words, how to deal appropriately with anger and intimidation.

Some parents teach their children violence:

- How to be mean.

- How to be nasty.

- How to be cruel.

- How to physically or emotionally hurt people.

There are not many really mean parents. But there are some. They beat their kids within an inch of their life. They teach their children to do the same to the next generation. If your parents are like that, you need help in not passing this violence on to the next generation. This is one lesson you should not learn from your parents.

Here's a typical example of how this intergenerational violence is learned:

When I first met Mike, age 14, he was in a juvenile lockup. The night before I came to see him, he had struck his mother repeatedly, breaking her jaw and two of her ribs. He told me that as a boy of 4 or 5 he watched his father beat his mother repeatedly. Then his dad abandoned the family. Mike said: "Once I got big enough, I followed my father's example with my mother. He got his way by hurting her. I thought I could, too."

If adults go around hitting people, screaming at them, shaking them, cursing, yelling, and hollering, their kids might tend to think: "Dad gets his needs met that way so maybe I can get my needs met that way, too."

# *Control* **Your Anger**

There are anger control methods galore. Many of them are well known:

- Taking "time out."

- Counting to 10.
- Deep breathing.
- Walking away.
- Talking it out with a friend.
- Taking it to prayer.

One thing is clear: The person who practices anger control successfully feels very good about himself or herself. Why? Because anger or intimidation are not in control of their lives. They are in control of their own lives. And self-governance and self-control lead to self-respect. You feel better about yourself.

# Avoid
*Horseplay*

Horseplay is very common. Avoid it.

- Sometimes it is "just kidding."

- But most of the time it is more than just kidding.

- It is subtle intimidation.

- Many, many fights among young people start with innocent-looking horseplay.

- The key is not to get involved in it.

- And the easiest way to do that is to walk away, whether it is at home or in your school.

# Avoid
## *Verbal Abuse*

Equally common is verbal intimidation.

- People use it to get their way.

- By hurting people.

- By making them the butt of jokes.

- By biting cynicism.

- By sniping.

- By carping.

Don't let cynicism get a toe-hold in your heart. The rule should be: "If you can't say something good, don't say anything at all."

Criticism and sarcasm take the warmth out of your life. Think of homes where this negative behavior is rampant. The kids in those homes feel unwelcome. They feel the coldness as soon as they enter. They have to be constantly on guard.

Also be careful lest you become a cause of violence by suggesting, "I'll get these two to fight and then enjoy it." Egging others on and then watching in glee as violence breaks out is as wrong as joining the fight yourself.

# What You *Can Do*

It is good to ask whether violence is an accepted part of your own and your family's way of dealing with one another. How often do these things happen in your home?

- Nonstop "nattering" or criticism.

- Constant insults.

- Too much horseplay.

- Violent outbursts.

- Throwing dishes.

- Smashing a window.

- Slugging a wall.

Can you, as the son or daughter in the family, take the lead in this regard? How about quietly talking to either Mom or Dad and asking if "we can have a family meeting" in order to reduce the violence in our own house?

- This request needs to be made at a time when the family is in a good mood, not a bad one.

- If you say it when everyone is in a bad mood, it will be counterproductive.

- It has to be said humbly, not arrogantly: "We all love our family. Can we sit down and talk about how to make it a better family?"

- You might start off by suggesting that everyone use the phrases "please" and "thank you" a lot more.

- And how about the phrase "I love you?"

We can develop an attitude and spirit within ourselves that are not a fertile ground for violence. Think of all the young people and their moms and dads who are successful in managing violent thoughts and impulses of their own and others.

What are these people like?

- They are honest and sensitive.

- They love their brothers and sisters and their children and their parents.

- They say their prayers every day.

- They work out their frustrations and resentments appropriately through anger control techniques.

- They are appropriately assertive so they can't be pushed around.

These skills and abilities can be learned. Just as you have seen others learn them, so, too, you can learn them yourself.

People with a temper usually justify it by saying: "I was born with a bad temper." If you say that, what you mean is: you do not intend to change and all the rest of us should learn to live with your terrible anger. That just doesn't seem fair.

On the other hand, you don't have to be a spoilsport either. We all learned when we were very young the difference between violence in reality and fantasy. *America's Funniest Home Videos* is a good example. A person falls off the bleachers, and nothing fatal happens. That's funny. It isn't funny if people are badly hurt or die. That's gruesome. We know that distinction. But we can help to reinforce it.

## Self-Defense

What about learning self-defense?

There are times when it is appropriate to defend yourself or someone else such as an innocent child or someone who cannot defend themselves. I know this seems like a gray area, and it doesn't seem like much of an issue. Why? Because most kids do tend to defend themselves. But some don't. So it is an issue.

The basic principle to remember is: Violence, even when legitimate, is a failure of everything else. It is giving up on negotiation or compromise, and it does have a price. Violence is not the first thing you should choose in self-defense and in defense of innocent victims. But it plays an important, yet minor role, especially in the management of our fears. You don't have to fear helplessly standing by and letting yourself or some innocent person be beaten mercilessly. There is something you can do. And that something even involves self-defense. Remember: The best offense is a good defense.

# Should You Join the Bullies?

Sometimes parents think that violence is present in our schools only when a student is badly beaten by other students or when one or more gun-carrying youth enter the building and proceed to blow others away.

Most students know differently. They realize that it is a culture of violence in an environment of bullying that makes a school violent all the time.

If, in your school, there are frequent and repeated threats to beat other kids up and that continues over and over again, then your school has a culture of violence.

All the bullies have to do is to beat one or two kids up and 99 others are afraid. For example, some primitive societies ran on threats of violence and reinforced those threats by periodic violent acts. If 10 people want something to eat and there is only one loaf of bread, the biggest guy, the fastest guy, or the meanest guy is going to get it. It is the way violent societies sort things out.

# Why Kids Become *Bullies*

Why do kids consider joining the bullies? Here are some reasons:

■ To join them is self-protection. "If I join the bullies, they can't beat me up."

- To join them is to get respect. "Other kids will be afraid of me now."

- All of us have a need for affection and affiliation. "If I join them, certain girls will be attracted to me."

- These are the benefits of membership in the bully club in school.

- These needs are met by joining the bullying club.

What are the entrance requirements to the bully club?

- You need to pay the admission price.

- You need to look like a bully and act like a bully to be accepted by the bullies.

- You need to respect them, and they will respect you.

- You need to be as mean as they are.

- Like a country club, it feels good that others are not allowed in the club because they are unworthy and inferior.

- The sales pitch for the bullying club is this: "We can simplify your life."

- "You want to be loyal. Here is the place that you can be loyal."

- "You want to be respected. Here is the place you will be respected."

- "You want to make sacrifices. Here is the place you can make sacrifices."

- "In our bullying club, there is team-work and loyalty."

- "We will even die for each other."

- This is a perverted way to do all of these things, but it is a way to get your needs met.

## Don't Be *Victimized*

How can you avoid being victimized by bullies? There are some simple things that any student can do to avoid being an object of violence by bullies:

- Don't attract their attention.

- Don't be smart with them.

- Stay away from their territory.

- Don't go looking for trouble.

- If you say, "I have a right to sit where I want and therefore I'll sit in your seat," you are looking for trouble.

- If you threaten them in any way, you are looking for trouble. Remember that bullies are very insecure.

- Also keep in mind that three out of four times a student is bullied, it could be avoided.

There are times, however, when crossing a bully's path is unavoidable.

- If you are bullied, you need to report it. Get some advice. In extreme cases, the enforcement authorities need to be notified.

■ The bottom line is this. Most bullying is "incidental bullying." That simply means that you stumble into their territory without realizing it and get threatened.

■ The best thing to do is to get out of their territory A.S.A.P.

■ Most incidental bullying goes away.

■ In adult life, we learn not to take walks in dangerous parts of the city at nighttime.

■ You need to learn not to take walks in certain parts of the school at any time.

■ There are times when we need to defend ourselves physically.

■ The best defense against bullying is not karate, but the smart behavior of not making yourself a target.

■ If you learn how to avoid making yourself a target as an adolescent, you can use those same skills when you are an adult.

There is a middle ground between joining the bullies on one hand, and being victimized by them on the other. That middle ground is a combination of avoiding trouble and finding friends instead who use self-respect, teamwork, and loyalty to help rather than hurt others. The need for affection and affiliation can be met in prosocial ways, and developing your friend-ship skills is a good start in that direction.

## Credits

| | |
|---|---|
| Production | Mary Steiner |
| Cover Design | Margie Brabec |
| Page Layout | Anne Hughes |

19-012
9907-19-0005